A kids' journal to record their birding experiences.

This NatureLog belongs to:

Special thanks to:
The great Bird Creator!
My parents, Marilyn and Ralph, for encouraging my creativity
My husband, Pete, for the support he provided
My children, Michael and Daniel, who always inspire me!

10 9 8 7 6
No part of this book may be reproduced by any means or in any form without the written permission of the publisher.

Published by:
Adventure Publications, Inc.
820 Cleveland St. S.
Cambridge, MN 55008
1-800-678-7006
www.adventurepublications.net

Printed and bound in the United States
Printed on recycled paper.

Cover and interior design/illustration:
DeAnna Brandt
Copy: DeAnna Brandt

ISBN-10: 1-885061-55-2
ISBN-13: 978-1-885061-55-3

Notice: The information contained in this book is true, complete, and accurate to the best of our knowledge.

All recommendations and suggestions are made without any guarantees on the part of the author or Adventure Publications, Inc.

The author and publisher disclaim all liability incurred in the connection with the use of this information. Neither the publisher nor the author shall be liable for any damage which may be caused or sustained as a result of the conduct of any of the activities in this book.

Log Tips

Record It!

As you explore the natural world around you, write down on the "Log" pages the birds you notice. Transfer the dates and names on those Log Pages to the Life List.

With the Life List included, you can record up to 32 birds! You can use this Log and Life List as a record of each different kind of bird you see, or write down every bird you see on a special day each year. For example: all the birds you see on Christmas day this year, then again next year, etc.

Check It Out!

You may want to look up your bird in a nature book, field guide, or on the internet to find out more about it. The National Audubon Society's web address is: www.audubon.org.

Be Creative!

Use the Photos/Art page to paste in your original artwork, a photograph you've taken or a postcard. Or, you may wish to use the space to glue a feather or piece of egg-shell you've found on the ground!

Have Fun!

Learn more with the bird "Facts". The "Games" are easy and can be done almost anywhere. Give back to the birds with the "Helps" ideas, explore with the "Try its".

Respect Nature!

Please leave things as you find them. Leave any eggs or babies in their nests or homes. If you find a baby out of the nest, leave it alone! The parents are probably waiting for you to leave so they can tend to it.

If you find a dead bird, be careful not to touch it, but use a stick to move it so you can observe more closely. If it has a band on it, make sure to record the number on it and call it in to your local nature center or Department of Natural Resources — they need this information about that bird!

Other Uses!

You don't have to be outside to use this log, go to the zoo, the natural history museum, science museum, or watch a movie or television program about birds.

Bird Parts

If you know the different parts of a bird, it's easier to identify them. This illustration shows the basic parts of a bird. It is a combination of many birds, not a real one.

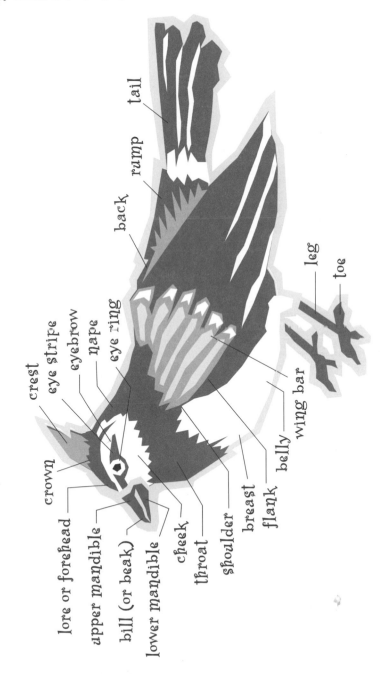

tail

rump

back

leg

toe

crest

eye stripe

eyebrow

nape

eye ring

wing bar

crown

belly

flank

breast

shoulder

throat

cheek

lower mandible

bill (or beak)

upper mandible

lore or forehead

Common Words

Bird of Prey: A hunting bird. Usually means the day-flying raptors, but sometimes refers to all birds that hunt prey generally larger than insects. This phrase is not usually used to describe insect-eating and fish-eating birds.

Call: A short sound or even a few notes usually used by a bird to tell other birds he's there, or that there's danger.

Carrion: Dead and decaying animals or their parts, eaten by birds (or other carrion eaters) that usually have not killed them.

Clutch: The set of eggs laid and taken care of by one parent or pair of birds at a time.

Color Phase: Different feather colors that distinguish some birds from others of the same species.

Display: The way a bird moves or presents itself to tell other birds when it wants to mate or when it wants to fight.

Down: A loose-textured, soft, fluffy feather or part of a feather, that helps insulate the body and retain heat.

Eye Ring: A narrow and differently colored ring of feathers or skin around the eye.

Eye Stripe: A differently colored stripe that goes across the side of the head including the area around the eye.

Forage: To look for any kind of food by hunting in an area.

Habitat: The type of natural place where a bird typically lives, for example: forest, swamp, shoreline, desert, etc.

Immature: A fully grown bird not old enough to breed, often with different feather colors than the adult. Another word for "Juvenile".

Incubation: To keep an egg warm, usually by the mother bird sitting on it, letting the chick inside grow.

Iridescent: The sparkling appearance of a feather. The feather structure makes it reflect light in such a way that it appears to be different colors.

Migratory: A type of bird that leaves an area and typically returns, either when the seasons change or to find food.

Mimicry: The ability of a bird to imitate sounds it hears, such as the songs and calls of other bird species, or occasionally other sounds, including the human voice.

Mobbing: Noisy calls and pretend attacks by a group of birds against another bird.

Molt: The process of shedding feathers. The feathers are usually replaced by new ones which may be of a different color or shape. This can happen before breeding, migration or when a change of season occurs.

Nestling: A very young bird that needs to remain in a nest and be tended by adults.

Preening: The action of a bird using its bill and/or claws to clean and groom its feathers.

Range: The area where a species of bird is typically found.

Roost: 1) To rest or sleep 2) A place where birds rest/sleep 3) a site where many birds roost.

Song: A series of sounds that a bird makes usually to declare its territory or to attract a mate.

Territory: An area defended by one or several birds, usually used for feeding and often for nesting. The area may be small, only surrounding one bird, or as much as several square miles.

Life List

	Date	Bird Name
1		
2		
3		
4		
5		
6		
7		
8		
9		
10		
11		
12		
13		
14		
15		

	Date	Bird Name
16	_____	_____
17	_____	_____
18	_____	_____
19	_____	_____
20	_____	_____
21	_____	_____
22	_____	_____
23	_____	_____
24	_____	_____
25	_____	_____
26	_____	_____
27	_____	_____
28	_____	_____
29	_____	_____
30	_____	_____
31	_____	_____
32	_____	_____

Log

Date/Time: _5/10/2023, 1:16 PM_

Season: _SUMMER_

Weather Conditions: _HOT, SUNNY_

_____

Bird Location: ☐ ground ☐ tree ☐ air
☐ phone wire ☒ other _FENCE_
How many are there? _1_

How big is the bird? _SMALL_

Any distinctive markings? _____

_____

What colors are on it? _BLUE &_
WHITE

_____

What shape are the wings?
☐ long ☒ short ☐ pointy ☐ round
☐ broad ☐ other _____

What does the tail look like?
☐ long ☐ short ☒ fanned ☐ forked
☐ straight ☐ other _____

What does the beak look like?
☐ thick ☒ pointy ☐ short ☐ long
☐ hooked   Color _BLACK_

Is there a band on its leg? _NO_

Name of bird I saw (enter this on your life list)

BLUE JAY

What is the bird doing? _SITTING_
ON FENCE

What does it sound like? _____

Is there a nest? Eggs? If so, describe:
_NO_
_____

Other interesting things I noticed:
_____
_____
_____

It looks like this:

Log

Date/Time: _____

Season: _____

Weather Conditions: _____

_____

Bird Location: ☐ ground   ☐ tree   ☐ air
☐ phone wire   ☐ other _____

How many are there? _____

How big is the bird? _____

Any distinctive markings? _____

_____

What colors are on it? _____

_____

_____

What shape are the wings?

☐ long   ☐ short   ☐ pointy   ☐ round
☐ broad   ☐ other _____

What does the tail look like?

☐ long   ☐ short   ☐ fanned   ☐ forked
☐ straight   ☐ other _____

What does the beak look like?

☐ thick   ☐ pointy   ☐ short   ☐ long
☐ hooked   Color _____

Is there a band on its leg? _____

Name of bird I saw (enter this on your life list)

What is the bird doing? _____

_____

What does it sound like? _____

_____

Is there a nest? Eggs? If so, describe:

_____

_____

Other interesting things I noticed:

_____

_____

_____

It looks like this:

Fact

The snowy egret's coloring is perfect for catching fish.

Its body is white so the fish doesn't see it as the bird wades in the water.

The fish is attracted to the bright yellow wormlike toes, comes closer to investigate, and is stabbed by the waiting egret.

Log

Date/Time: _____

Season: _____

Weather Conditions: _____

_____

Bird Location: ☐ ground ☐ tree ☐ air
☐ phone wire ☐ other _____

How many are there? _____

How big is the bird? _____

Any distinctive markings? _____

_____

What colors are on it? _____

_____

_____

What shape are the wings?

☐ long ☐ short ☐ pointy ☐ round
☐ broad ☐ other _____

What does the tail look like?

☐ long ☐ short ☐ fanned ☐ forked
☐ straight ☐ other _____

What does the beak look like?

☐ thick ☐ pointy ☐ short ☐ long
☐ hooked   Color _____

Is there a band on its leg? _____

Name of bird I saw (enter this on your life list)

What is the bird doing? _____

_____

What does it sound like? _____

_____

Is there a nest? Eggs? If so, describe:

_____

_____

Other interesting things I noticed:

_____

_____

_____

It looks like this:

Fact

Flamingos eat from salty, muddy water.

They feed with their heads held upside down sweeping their bills through the water.

As their beaks fill up with water, the fine filter system inside their bills keeps the tiny shrimp and water plants in but lets the water run out.

What remains in their bill becomes their dinner.

Log

Date/Time: _____

Season: _____

Weather Conditions: _____

_____

Bird Location: ☐ ground ☐ tree ☐ air
☐ phone wire ☐ other _____

How many are there? _____

How big is the bird? _____

Any distinctive markings? _____

_____

What colors are on it? _____

_____

_____

What shape are the wings?
☐ long ☐ short ☐ pointy ☐ round
☐ broad ☐ other _____

What does the tail look like?
☐ long ☐ short ☐ fanned ☐ forked
☐ straight ☐ other _____

What does the beak look like?
☐ thick ☐ pointy ☐ short ☐ long
☐ hooked   Color _____

Is there a band on its leg? _____

Name of bird I saw (enter this on your life list)

What is the bird doing? _____

_____

What does it sound like? _____

_____

Is there a nest? Eggs? If so, describe:

_____

_____

Other interesting things I noticed:

_____

_____

_____

It looks like this:

Log

Date/Time: _____

Season: _____

Weather Conditions: _____
_____

Bird Location: ☐ ground ☐ tree ☐ air
☐ phone wire ☐ other _____

How many are there? _____

How big is the bird? _____

Any distinctive markings? _____
_____

What colors are on it? _____
_____
_____

What shape are the wings?
☐ long ☐ short ☐ pointy ☐ round
☐ broad ☐ other _____

What does the tail look like?
☐ long ☐ short ☐ fanned ☐ forked
☐ straight ☐ other _____

What does the beak look like?
☐ thick ☐ pointy ☐ short ☐ long
☐ hooked   Color _____

Is there a band on its leg? _____

Name of bird I saw (enter this on your life list)

What is the bird doing? _____

_____

What does it sound like? _____

_____

Is there a nest? Eggs? If so, describe:

_____

_____

Other interesting things I noticed:

_____

_____

_____

It looks like this:

Log

Date/Time: _____

Season: _____

Weather Conditions: _____
_____

Bird Location: ☐ ground ☐ tree ☐ air
☐ phone wire ☐ other _____

How many are there? _____

How big is the bird? _____

Any distinctive markings? _____
_____

What colors are on it? _____
_____
_____

What shape are the wings?
☐ long ☐ short ☐ pointy ☐ round ◄
☐ broad ☐ other _____ ◄

What does the tail look like?
☐ long ☐ short ☐ fanned ☐ forked
☐ straight ☐ other_____

What does the beak look like?
☐ thick ☐ pointy ☐ short ☐ long
☐ hooked   Color _____

Is there a band on its leg? _____

Name of bird I saw (enter this on your life list)

What is the bird doing? _____

_____

What does it sound like? _____

_____

Is there a nest? Eggs? If so, describe:

_____

_____

Other interesting things I noticed:

_____

_____

_____

It looks like this:

Try it

Start collecting stamps that have pictures of birds on them.

Go to your local post office and ask if they have any bird stamps, look in hobby shops, or have long distance friends and relatives send bird stamps on their letters to you.

Log

Date/Time: _____

Season: _____

Weather Conditions: _____

_____

Bird Location: ☐ ground ☐ tree ☐ air
☐ phone wire ☐ other _____

How many are there? _____

How big is the bird? _____

Any distinctive markings? _____

_____

What colors are on it? _____

_____

_____

What shape are the wings?
☐ long ☐ short ☐ pointy ☐ round
☐ broad ☐ other _____

What does the tail look like?
☐ long ☐ short ☐ fanned ☐ forked
☐ straight ☐ other _____

What does the beak look like?
☐ thick ☐ pointy ☐ short ☐ long
☐ hooked   Color _____

Is there a band on its leg? _____

Name of bird I saw (enter this on your life list)

What is the bird doing? _____

_____

What does it sound like? _____

_____

Is there a nest? Eggs? If so, describe:

_____

_____

Other interesting things I noticed:

_____

_____

_____

It looks like this:

Frigatebirds do not always find food on their own – they usually steal it.

They fly after other seabirds and bully them into dropping their catch of fish in midair.

Then the frigatebirds dive to catch the food before it lands in the sea.

Log

Date/Time: _____

Season: _____

Weather Conditions: _____
_____

Bird Location: ☐ ground   ☐ tree   ☐ air
☐ phone wire ☐ other _____

How many are there? _____

How big is the bird? _____

Any distinctive markings? _____
_____

What colors are on it? _____
_____
_____

What shape are the wings?
☐ long   ☐ short   ☐ pointy ☐ round
☐ broad   ☐ other _____

What does the tail look like?
☐ long   ☐ short   ☐ fanned ☐ forked
☐ straight ☐ other_____

What does the beak look like?
☐ thick   ☐ pointy   ☐ short   ☐ long
☐ hooked   Color _____

Is there a band on its leg?_____

Name of bird I saw (enter this on your life list)

What is the bird doing? _____

_____

What does it sound like? _____

_____

Is there a nest? Eggs? If so, describe:

_____

_____

Other interesting things I noticed:

_____

_____

_____

It looks like this:

Log

Date/Time: _____

Season: _____

Weather Conditions: _____

_____

Bird Location: ☐ ground   ☐ tree   ☐ air
☐ phone wire   ☐ other _____

How many are there? _____

How big is the bird? _____

Any distinctive markings? _____

_____

What colors are on it? _____

_____

_____

What shape are the wings?
☐ long   ☐ short   ☐ pointy   ☐ round
☐ broad   ☐ other _____

What does the tail look like?
☐ long   ☐ short   ☐ fanned   ☐ forked
☐ straight   ☐ other_____

What does the beak look like?
☐ thick   ☐ pointy   ☐ short   ☐ long
☐ hooked   Color _____

Is there a band on its leg?_____

Name of bird I saw (enter this on your life list)

What is the bird doing? _____

_____

What does it sound like? _____

_____

Is there a nest? Eggs? If so, describe:

_____

_____

Other interesting things I noticed:

_____

_____

_____

It looks like this:

Log

Date/Time: _____

Season: _____

Weather Conditions: _____

_____

Bird Location: ☐ ground   ☐ tree   ☐ air
☐ phone wire   ☐ other _____

How many are there? _____

How big is the bird? _____

Any distinctive markings? _____

_____

What colors are on it? _____

_____

_____

What shape are the wings?
☐ long   ☐ short   ☐ pointy   ☐ round
☐ broad   ☐ other _____

What does the tail look like?
☐ long   ☐ short   ☐ fanned   ☐ forked
☐ straight   ☐ other _____

What does the beak look like?
☐ thick   ☐ pointy   ☐ short   ☐ long
☐ hooked   Color _____

Is there a band on its leg? _____

Name of bird I saw (enter this on your life list)

What is the bird doing? _____

_____

What does it sound like? _____

_____

Is there a nest? Eggs? If so, describe:

_____

_____

Other interesting things I noticed:

_____

_____

_____

It looks like this:

Log

Date/Time: _____

Season: _____

Weather Conditions: _____

_____

Bird Location: ☐ ground   ☐ tree   ☐ air
☐ phone wire   ☐ other _____

How many are there? _____

How big is the bird? _____

Any distinctive markings? _____

_____

What colors are on it? _____

_____

_____

What shape are the wings?
☐ long   ☐ short   ☐ pointy   ☐ round
☐ broad   ☐ other _____

What does the tail look like?
☐ long   ☐ short   ☐ fanned   ☐ forked
☐ straight   ☐ other _____

What does the beak look like?
☐ thick   ☐ pointy   ☐ short   ☐ long
☐ hooked   Color _____

Is there a band on its leg? _____

Name of bird I saw (enter this on your life list)

What is the bird doing? _____

_____

What does it sound like? _____

_____

Is there a nest? Eggs? If so, describe:

_____

_____

Other interesting things I noticed:

_____

_____

_____

It looks like this:

Fact

Many birds, including chickadees, act as toilet flushers.

Their babies' droppings come out in bags called fecal sacs.

Immediately the parents take the sacs, fly away and drop them.

Getting rid of the white droppings keeps the nest and babies clean and makes it more difficult for enemies to find the nest.

Log

Date/Time: _____

Season: _____

Weather Conditions: _____
_____

Bird Location: ☐ ground ☐ tree ☐ air
☐ phone wire ☐ other _____

How many are there? _____

How big is the bird? _____

Any distinctive markings? _____
_____

What colors are on it? _____
_____
_____

What shape are the wings?
☐ long ☐ short ☐ pointy ☐ round
☐ broad ☐ other _____

What does the tail look like?
☐ long ☐ short ☐ fanned ☐ forked
☐ straight ☐ other _____

What does the beak look like?
☐ thick ☐ pointy ☐ short ☐ long
☐ hooked   Color _____

Is there a band on its leg? _____

Name of bird I saw (enter this on your life list)

What is the bird doing? _____

_____

What does it sound like? _____

_____

Is there a nest? Eggs? If so, describe:

_____

_____

Other interesting things I noticed:

_____

_____

_____

It looks like this:

Game

Name that bird!

One person writes down the name of a bird that the other person has to guess.

The guesser tries to ask as few questions as possible in order to name that bird.

They may even get it right after only one question!

Switch places and see how many questions the other person needs to ask before guessing the bird.

Log

Date/Time: _____

Season: _____

Weather Conditions: _____
_____

Bird Location: ☐ ground   ☐ tree   ☐ air
☐ phone wire   ☐ other _____

How many are there? _____

How big is the bird? _____

Any distinctive markings? _____
_____

What colors are on it? _____
_____
_____

What shape are the wings?
☐ long   ☐ short   ☐ pointy ☐ round
☐ broad   ☐ other _____

What does the tail look like?
☐ long   ☐ short   ☐ fanned ☐ forked
☐ straight   ☐ other _____

What does the beak look like?
☐ thick   ☐ pointy ☐ short   ☐ long
☐ hooked   Color _____

Is there a band on its leg? _____

Name of bird I saw (enter this on your life list)

What is the bird doing? _____

_____

What does it sound like? _____

_____

Is there a nest? Eggs? If so, describe:

_____

_____

Other interesting things I noticed:

_____

_____

_____

It looks like this:

Log

Date/Time: _____

Season: _____

Weather Conditions: _____

_____

Bird Location: ☐ ground   ☐ tree   ☐ air
☐ phone wire ☐ other _____

How many are there? _____

How big is the bird? _____

Any distinctive markings? _____

_____

What colors are on it? _____

_____

_____

What shape are the wings?
☐ long   ☐ short   ☐ pointy ☐ round
☐ broad   ☐ other _____

What does the tail look like?
☐ long   ☐ short   ☐ fanned ☐ forked
☐ straight ☐ other_____

What does the beak look like?
☐ thick   ☐ pointy ☐ short   ☐ long
☐ hooked   Color _____

Is there a band on its leg?_____

What is the bird doing? _____

_____

What does it sound like? _____

_____

Is there a nest? Eggs? If so, describe:

_____

_____

Other interesting things I noticed:

_____

_____

_____

It looks like this:

Fact

White pelicans often capture fish cooperatively.

They form a long line, beat their wings and drive the prey into shallow water, where they seize the fish in their large, pouched bills.

Log

Date/Time: _____

Season: _____

Weather Conditions: _____
_____

Bird Location: ☐ ground   ☐ tree   ☐ air
☐ phone wire ☐ other _____

How many are there? _____

How big is the bird? _____

Any distinctive markings? _____
_____

What colors are on it? _____
_____
_____

What shape are the wings?
☐ long   ☐ short   ☐ pointy ☐ round
☐ broad ☐ other _____

What does the tail look like?
☐ long   ☐ short   ☐ fanned ☐ forked
☐ straight ☐ other_____

What does the beak look like?
☐ thick   ☐ pointy   ☐ short   ☐ long
☐ hooked   Color _____

Is there a band on its leg?_____

What is the bird doing? _____

_____

What does it sound like? _____

_____

Is there a nest? Eggs? If so, describe:

_____

_____

Other interesting things I noticed:

_____

_____

_____

It looks like this:

Fact

Birds cannot sweat when they get hot.

They *usually* just pant but they can bathe, find shade and ruffle their feathers to let heat escape.

Turkey vultures let their droppings dribble down their legs when they're overheated.

As the wetness evaporates, it cools them off just as sweat would.

Log

Date/Time: _____

Season: _____

Weather Conditions: _____

_____

Bird Location: ☐ ground ☐ tree ☐ air
☐ phone wire ☐ other _____

How many are there? _____

How big is the bird? _____

Any distinctive markings? _____

_____

What colors are on it? _____

_____

_____

What shape are the wings?

☐ long ☐ short ☐ pointy ☐ round
☐ broad ☐ other _____

What does the tail look like?

☐ long ☐ short ☐ fanned ☐ forked
☐ straight ☐ other_____

What does the beak look like?

☐ thick ☐ pointy ☐ short ☐ long
☐ hooked Color _____

Is there a band on its leg? _____

Name of bird I saw (enter this on your life list)

What is the bird doing? _____

_____

What does it sound like? _____

_____

Is there a nest? Eggs? If so, describe:

_____

_____

Other interesting things I noticed:

_____

_____

_____

It looks like this:

Log

Date/Time: _____

Season: _____

Weather Conditions: _____

_____

Bird Location: ☐ ground ☐ tree ☐ air
☐ phone wire ☐ other _____

How many are there? _____

How big is the bird? _____

Any distinctive markings? _____

_____

What colors are on it? _____

_____

_____

What shape are the wings?
☐ long ☐ short ☐ pointy ☐ round
☐ broad ☐ other _____

What does the tail look like?
☐ long ☐ short ☐ fanned ☐ forked
☐ straight ☐ other_____

What does the beak look like?
☐ thick ☐ pointy ☐ short ☐ long
☐ hooked   Color_____

Is there a band on its leg?_____

What is the bird doing? _____

_____

What does it sound like? _____

_____

Is there a nest? Eggs? If so, describe:

_____

_____

Other interesting things I noticed:

_____

_____

_____

It looks like this:

Fact

A peacock's beautiful long feathers are not its tail feathers but ones that grow out of its back.

Its tail feathers are behind the fan, and they stand up stiff and straight to help hold it up.

Young males practice lifting their feathers long before they have a big feather fan to hold up, which happens when they're about 6 years old.

Log

Date/Time: _____

Season: _____

Weather Conditions: _____

_____

Bird Location: ☐ ground ☐ tree ☐ air
☐ phone wire ☐ other _____

How many are there? _____

How big is the bird? _____

Any distinctive markings? _____

_____

What colors are on it? _____

_____

_____

What shape are the wings?
☐ long ☐ short ☐ pointy ☐ round
☐ broad ☐ other _____

What does the tail look like?
☐ long ☐ short ☐ fanned ☐ forked
☐ straight ☐ other _____

What does the beak look like?
☐ thick ☐ pointy ☐ short ☐ long
☐ hooked   Color _____

Is there a band on its leg? _____

Name of bird I saw (enter this on your life list)

What is the bird doing? _____

_____

What does it sound like? _____

_____

Is there a nest? Eggs? If so, describe:

_____

_____

Other interesting things I noticed:

_____

_____

_____

It looks like this:

Helps

Feed the birds!

If you don't have a birdfeeder, you can simply sprinkle birdseed or breadcrumbs on the ground or on a flat rock, pack a pinecone with peanut butter and roll in seeds and hang from a tree, or nail a half an orange or coconut to a tree.

41

Log

Date/Time: _____

Season: _____

Weather Conditions: _____
_____

Bird Location: ☐ ground ☐ tree ☐ air
☐ phone wire ☐ other _____
How many are there? _____

How big is the bird? _____
Any distinctive markings? _____
_____

What colors are on it? _____
_____
_____

What shape are the wings?
☐ long ☐ short ☐ pointy ☐ round
☐ broad ☐ other _____

What does the tail look like?
☐ long ☐ short ☐ fanned ☐ forked
☐ straight ☐ other _____

What does the beak look like?
☐ thick ☐ pointy ☐ short ☐ long
☐ hooked   Color _____

Is there a band on its leg? _____

What is the bird doing? _____

_____

What does it sound like? _____

_____

Is there a nest? Eggs? If so, describe:

_____

_____

Other interesting things I noticed:

_____

_____

_____

It looks like this:

Fact

A peregrine falcon during a dive is faster than a cheetah running at full speed.

In their downward plunge, peregrines can reach speeds of more than 100 miles per hour.

Even when flying level, they often fly as fast as 75 miles per hour.

Cheetahs can run about 65 to 70 miles per hour.

Log

Date/Time: _____

Season: _____

Weather Conditions: _____
_____

Bird Location: ☐ ground ☐ tree ☐ air
☐ phone wire ☐ other _____

How many are there? _____

How big is the bird? _____

Any distinctive markings? _____
_____

What colors are on it? _____
_____
_____

What shape are the wings?
☐ long ☐ short ☐ pointy ☐ round
☐ broad ☐ other _____

What does the tail look like?
☐ long ☐ short ☐ fanned ☐ forked
☐ straight ☐ other_____

What does the beak look like?
☐ thick ☐ pointy ☐ short ☐ long
☐ hooked   Color _____

Is there a band on its leg?_____

What is the bird doing? _____

_____

What does it sound like? _____

_____

Is there a nest? Eggs? If so, describe:

_____

_____

Other interesting things I noticed:

_____

_____

_____

It looks like this:

Log

Date/Time: _____

Season: _____

Weather Conditions: _____
_____

Bird Location: ☐ ground ☐ tree ☐ air
☐ phone wire ☐ other _____

How many are there? _____

How big is the bird? _____

Any distinctive markings? _____
_____

What colors are on it? _____
_____
_____

What shape are the wings?
☐ long ☐ short ☐ pointy ☐ round
☐ broad ☐ other _____

What does the tail look like?
☐ long ☐ short ☐ fanned ☐ forked
☐ straight ☐ other_____

What does the beak look like?
☐ thick ☐ pointy ☐ short ☐ long
☐ hooked   Color _____

Is there a band on its leg?_____

Name of bird I saw (enter this on your life list)

What is the bird doing? _____

_____

What does it sound like? _____

_____

Is there a nest? Eggs? If so, describe:

_____

_____

Other interesting things I noticed:

_____

_____

_____

It looks like this:

Fact

Red-cockaded woodpeckers don't make nest holes in dead trees the way most woodpeckers do – they go for live pine trees.

Sticky sap oozes out of the main nest hole and the other nearby holes that the bird pecks.

The sap helps keep snakes from climbing to the hole and eating the eggs and babies.

Log

Date/Time: _____

Season: _____

Weather Conditions: _____

_____

Bird Location: ☐ ground   ☐ tree   ☐ air
☐ phone wire ☐ other _____

How many are there? _____

How big is the bird? _____

Any distinctive markings? _____

_____

What colors are on it? _____

_____

_____

What shape are the wings?
☐ long   ☐ short   ☐ pointy ☐ round
☐ broad   ☐ other _____

What does the tail look like?
☐ long   ☐ short   ☐ fanned ☐ forked
☐ straight ☐ other_____

What does the beak look like?
☐ thick   ☐ pointy ☐ short   ☐ long
☐ hooked   Color _____

Is there a band on its leg?_____

Name of bird I saw (enter this on your life list)

What is the bird doing? _____

_____

What does it sound like? _____

_____

Is there a nest? Eggs? If so, describe:

_____

_____

Other interesting things I noticed:

_____

_____

_____

It looks like this:

Fact

The cardinal is the official state bird for 7 states in the United States.

They are Illinois, Indiana, Kentucky, North Carolina, Ohio, Virginia, and West Virginia.

Three of the 10 Canadian provinces have owls as their provincial bird.

They are: Alberta — the great horned owl, Quebec — the snowy owl, and Manitoba — the great grey owl.

Log

Date/Time: _____

Season: _____

Weather Conditions: _____

_____

Bird Location: ☐ ground   ☐ tree   ☐ air
☐ phone wire   ☐ other _____

How many are there? _____

How big is the bird? _____

Any distinctive markings? _____

_____

What colors are on it? _____

_____

_____

What shape are the wings?

☐ long   ☐ short   ☐ pointy   ☐ round
☐ broad   ☐ other _____

What does the tail look like?

☐ long   ☐ short   ☐ fanned   ☐ forked
☐ straight   ☐ other_____

What does the beak look like?

☐ thick   ☐ pointy   ☐ short   ☐ long
☐ hooked   Color _____

Is there a band on its leg?_____

Name of bird I saw (enter this on your life list)

What is the bird doing? _____

_____

What does it sound like? _____

_____

Is there a nest? Eggs? If so, describe:

_____

_____

Other interesting things I noticed:

_____

_____

_____

It looks like this:

Fact

More than 200 kinds of birds let ants run through their feathers.

Scientists call this "anting."

They spread their wings over ant hills and let the ants run all over their bodies or they pick up the ants and put them among their feathers or rub them against their skin.

Ants give off a chemical that seems to keep some tiny pests away or even kill them.

Log

Date/Time: _____

Season: _____

Weather Conditions: _____
_____

Bird Location: ☐ ground   ☐ tree   ☐ air
☐ phone wire   ☐ other _____

How many are there? _____

How big is the bird? _____

Any distinctive markings? _____
_____

What colors are on it? _____
_____
_____

What shape are the wings?
☐ long   ☐ short   ☐ pointy   ☐ round
☐ broad   ☐ other _____

What does the tail look like?
☐ long   ☐ short   ☐ fanned   ☐ forked
☐ straight   ☐ other _____

What does the beak look like?
☐ thick   ☐ pointy   ☐ short   ☐ long
☐ hooked   Color _____

Is there a band on its leg? _____

Name of bird I saw (enter this on your life list)

What is the bird doing? _____

_____

What does it sound like? _____

_____

Is there a nest? Eggs? If so, describe:

_____

_____

Other interesting things I noticed:

_____

_____

_____

It looks like this:

Try it

Practice drawing birds.

Look at photos in magazines, books, or field guides.

Check out library books about drawing birds.

Draw the birds that you see outside or at the zoo.

Keep an art journal and watch your progression.

This will also give you keener observation skills for birdwatching.

Log

Date/Time: _____

Season: _____

Weather Conditions: _____
_____

Bird Location: ☐ ground   ☐ tree   ☐ air
☐ phone wire   ☐ other _____

How many are there? _____

How big is the bird? _____

Any distinctive markings? _____
_____

What colors are on it? _____
_____
_____

What shape are the wings?
☐ long   ☐ short   ☐ pointy   ☐ round
☐ broad   ☐ other _____

What does the tail look like?
☐ long   ☐ short   ☐ fanned   ☐ forked
☐ straight   ☐ other _____

What does the beak look like?
☐ thick   ☐ pointy   ☐ short   ☐ long
☐ hooked   Color _____

Is there a band on its leg? _____

What is the bird doing? _____

_____

What does it sound like? _____

_____

Is there a nest? Eggs? If so, describe:

_____

_____

Other interesting things I noticed:

_____

_____

_____

It looks like this:

Fact

The ostrich is the largest bird in the world.

It can grow up to 9 feet tall.

The smallest bird is the bee hummingbird of Cuba, which is no larger than a bumblebee.

The heaviest flying bird ever recorded was a mute swan that weighed 50 pounds.

Log

Date/Time: _____

Season: _____

Weather Conditions: _____
_____

Bird Location: ☐ ground ☐ tree ☐ air
☐ phone wire ☐ other _____

How many are there? _____

How big is the bird? _____

Any distinctive markings? _____
_____

What colors are on it? _____
_____
_____

What shape are the wings?
☐ long ☐ short ☐ pointy ☐ round
☐ broad ☐ other _____

What does the tail look like?
☐ long ☐ short ☐ fanned ☐ forked
☐ straight ☐ other_____

What does the beak look like?
☐ thick ☐ pointy ☐ short ☐ long
☐ hooked Color _____

Is there a band on its leg?_____

Name of bird I saw (enter this on your life list)

What is the bird doing? _____

_____

What does it sound like? _____

_____

Is there a nest? Eggs? If so, describe:

_____

_____

Other interesting things I noticed:

_____

_____

_____

It looks like this:

Log

Date/Time: _____

Season: _____

Weather Conditions: _____
_____

Bird Location: ☐ ground ☐ tree ☐ air
☐ phone wire ☐ other _____

How many are there? _____

How big is the bird? _____

Any distinctive markings? _____
_____

What colors are on it? _____
_____
_____

What shape are the wings?
☐ long ☐ short ☐ pointy ☐ round
☐ broad ☐ other _____

What does the tail look like?
☐ long ☐ short ☐ fanned ☐ forked
☐ straight ☐ other _____

What does the beak look like?
☐ thick ☐ pointy ☐ short ☐ long
☐ hooked Color _____

Is there a band on its leg? _____

Name of bird I saw (enter this on your life list)

What is the bird doing? _____

_____

What does it sound like? _____

_____

Is there a nest? Eggs? If so, describe:

_____

_____

Other interesting things I noticed:

_____

_____

_____

It looks like this:

Fact

You may see robins cocking their heads as if they are listening for worms.

Experiments have shown that these songbirds find worms by sight, not by sound.

Since their eyes are on the sides of their heads, the cocking enables them to see the worms better.

Log

Date/Time: _____

Season: _____

Weather Conditions: _____
_____

Bird Location: ☐ ground ☐ tree ☐ air
☐ phone wire ☐ other _____

How many are there? _____

How big is the bird? _____

Any distinctive markings? _____
_____

What colors are on it? _____
_____
_____

What shape are the wings?
☐ long ☐ short ☐ pointy ☐ round
☐ broad ☐ other _____

What does the tail look like?
☐ long ☐ short ☐ fanned ☐ forked
☐ straight ☐ other _____

What does the beak look like?
☐ thick ☐ pointy ☐ short ☐ long
☐ hooked   Color _____

Is there a band on its leg? _____

Name of bird I saw (enter this on your life list)

What is the bird doing? _____

_____

What does it sound like? _____

_____

Is there a nest? Eggs? If so, describe:

_____

_____

Other interesting things I noticed:

_____

_____

_____

It looks like this:

Log

Date/Time: _____

Season: _____

Weather Conditions: _____

_____

Bird Location: ☐ ground ☐ tree ☐ air
☐ phone wire ☐ other _____

How many are there? _____

How big is the bird? _____

Any distinctive markings? _____

_____

What colors are on it? _____

_____

_____

What shape are the wings?
☐ long ☐ short ☐ pointy ☐ round
☐ broad ☐ other _____

What does the tail look like?
☐ long ☐ short ☐ fanned ☐ forked
☐ straight ☐ other _____

What does the beak look like?
☐ thick ☐ pointy ☐ short ☐ long
☐ hooked Color _____

Is there a band on its leg? _____

What is the bird doing? _____

_____

What does it sound like? _____

_____

Is there a nest? Eggs? If so, describe:

_____

_____

Other interesting things I noticed:

_____

_____

_____

It looks like this:

Fact

Hornbills make their nests in holes in tree trunks.

When the female is settled on the eggs, the male builds a wall in front of the hole, leaving a small opening to feed her and their young.

When they are partly grown, the female leaves the nest and the young re-build the wall and both the mom and dad birds continue to feed the young until they are old enough to leave.

Log

Date/Time: _____

Season: _____

Weather Conditions: _____
_____

Bird Location: ☐ ground ☐ tree ☐ air
☐ phone wire ☐ other _____

How many are there? _____

How big is the bird? _____

Any distinctive markings? _____
_____

What colors are on it? _____
_____
_____

What shape are the wings?
☐ long ☐ short ☐ pointy ☐ round
☐ broad ☐ other _____

What does the tail look like?
☐ long ☐ short ☐ fanned ☐ forked
☐ straight ☐ other _____

What does the beak look like?
☐ thick ☐ pointy ☐ short ☐ long
☐ hooked Color _____

Is there a band on its leg? _____

Name of bird I saw (enter this on your life list)

What is the bird doing? _____

_____

What does it sound like? _____

_____

Is there a nest? Eggs? If so, describe:

_____

_____

Other interesting things I noticed:

_____

_____

_____

It looks like this:

Game

Make up a new kind of bird, using parts of at least three different birds.

Draw a picture of it and give it a name.

Write about it. Some ideas: what it eats, how it gets its food, where it lives, if it has a nest, what sound it makes, what the eggs/chicks look like, if it migrates, if the female has different colors or features.

Photo/Art

Date: _____ Description: _____
_____

Photo/Art

Date: _____ Description: _____
_____

Photo/Art

Date: _____   Description: _____

_____

Photo/Art

Date: _____ Description: _____

_____

Photo/Art

Date: _____ Description: _____
_____

Photo/Art

Date: _____ Description: _____
_____

Photo/Art

Date: _____   Description: _____
_____

Photo/Art

Date: _____ Description: _____

_____

Photo/Art

Date: _____ Description: _____
_____

Photo/Art

Date: _____ Description: _____

_____

Photo/Art

Date: _____ Description: _____
_____

Index

Index

Use this page to record what's on
your personal Photos/Art Pages

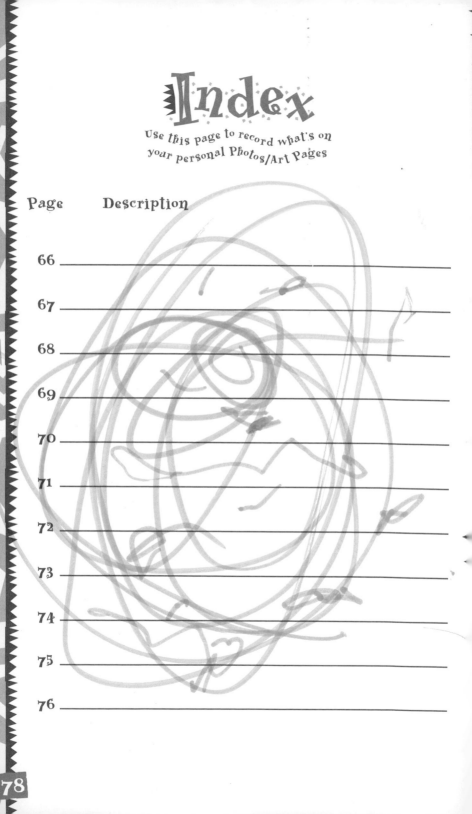

Page	Description
66	
67	
68	
69	
70	
71	
72	
73	
74	
75	
76	